T0090475

A book of Revelations from Jesus to a young Woman who found Jesus

MS DONNA L HOWARD

authorHOUSE°

AuthorHouse™
1663 Liberty Drive
Bloomington, IN 47403
www.authorhouse.com
Phone: 833-262-8899

Published by AuthorHouse 06/23/2023

ISBN: 979-8-8230-0178-6 (sc)
ISBN: 979-8-8230-0177-9 (e)

Print information available on the last page.

This book is printed on acid-free paper.

CONTENTS

INTRODUCTION

All of these stories that you are about to read, are truth and fact. For I, this young woman, experienced these events, and God was with me through it all; even until the end of time....

Praise be to God

A Precious Child Of God
Who had became born into the world

Year of 1965

A PRECIOUS CHILD OF GOD

Once upon a time There was This Precious child of God who had Become Born into the world little did she no that she would Experience all kinds of life turning Events] such as talking to God at a very Small age The age of Five to be Exact land when in time of need such as protection 'afraid' lonely and boredom' this little child wood look out the

Window and start to pray' as she prayed she would see God surface' each and every time before her very eyes so you may ask what did God look like to the very small child / well he looked very Giant and his Entire Body was that of a Radiant Glowing Light] but the little girl was never afraid because the Lord God would Comfort her in such an awesome way' and his Magnificent Spirit would let her no that she indeed was safe because God had Manifest himself before her very eyes in such a Marvelous way Amen

That she knew that she was safe and protected when ever this child asked for help in anyway God made it the help that is Surrounded her One day the small child asked God to deliver her out of the hands of where she was being raised but little did the child no that all of her Trials would began to start to surround her but this Amazing God Truly never ever left her side there had become a time that the child was sent places like

Foster homes as she had gotten older she was sent to Group homes in which the young girl was so gifted and Talented the young girl Experience Modeling] Acting] Singing in every single thing she had experience the girl had very Supperve Expertise in every thing she did in other words she was an Expert at what she did not to Mention Writing this young

Girl realized that God had showed her she could one day come to live a life rather then The poor poverty life style she had been used too one day while writing a Composition story as home work her school teacher said to prepare on why i Love my parents well this young girl father had past away] But this Gifted girl wrote about how she Loved her Foster Mother and said the reason why was because she may have not been with her Mother but she was proud and grateful for having such a person to call her mother Amen now the girl also experience situations like being bullied as well from boys at school mocking her but the Holy Spirit said

To her God that is Listen my child you are indeed my Precious child] and Fret not so on the day of recital the young girl walked upon the stage and read why she loved her parents and was giving a standing ovation for hers the girl that is was the best written story out of her Entire classmates and the young girl foster mother was giving a plaque for the outstanding work of the young girls great work and performance Remember if they that Mocked Jesus they who Dare's will also Mock someone that they can see the Light of God that Shines within them Amen Hallelujah Praise be to God This gave the young girl strength to carry on and not be discourage in anyway because God said Precede these words that no matter what there is no Weapon formed against you Shall Prosper WOwww] so the girl went with that Continually in her Spirit

Knowing that God was her all time and forever lasting protection Amen as cant no one touch what God has set forth 'Amen and there that fine day that Graduation came with the young girls done so beautifully graduating from jr high school the young girl walked across that stage with so much joy and achievement' she was proud of her own self wow she said to her self God is so good to me Amen thank you Jesus 'now things couldn't get even better when she started attending Church at a very young age' ooh yes indeed things got better they actually had gotten Great and one Beautiful Day she decided to become Baptized in the Holy water and the Holy Blood of Jesus and the Holy Spirit of God in Heaven the young Female was indeed Baptized on this Beautiful Sunday mourning and when the Pastor said Before all

The church Members' he said he wanted all of the five people who had been Baptized this Sunday to come step before the Hole Church Congregation and say each one out loud here I stand and have Given My SOUL and very Life to God as Ive been Baptized in His Holy Spirit 'Amen Again But Amazingly when the young woman said Those words everybody began to stand and say one after another Ooh Glory be to God That young Female has the Light of God upon her and it surrounds her Entire Body We can see it Out loud to the Pastor they all applaused her with the most utmost Glorifying standing Ovation and said to the young woman and where ever you Should go in Life people Will see this Marvelous Light of God that Shines upon you and that she was Truly a Great Inspiration to others Especially those who maybe struggling to find Christ in there Lives Amen again and Lets all Praise his Holy Name Hallelujah

Father God it is your Grace and Mercy that Brings us forward in your gracious will and your way and with that being said done the young Precious Child of God is now a Adult Woman and she indeed has began to Prosper Successfully' still writing her original songs and Books the Almighty God has proven himself in all these Joys' keeping her with a sound mind' health; and even Love all these things have been made Manifested because of all the Patience this young Child had and kept her Faith in God Thee most Utmost' Awesome' Greatest hes Glorifying his Mercy' his Grace' and so with that all these things we Honor and Magnify his Holy Blessed Name Amen Father God we Love you because of your Unconditional Loving Care Grace and concerns for all of us we are your Precious Children of you Our Almighty God and so Ends this

Story as the little Sparrow watchet over her the Moral of this Story is that God will Land you all things in your Life if you will only seek patients and Believeth in him even if your just a little Precious Child of God in Jesus Name Amen

No Weapon Formed Against you Shall Prosper
Isaiah 54 King James Version Holy Bible

Amen Jesus

A Generational Curse
The slave Masters Wife Could Not
Make Or Produce Milk

Year of 1926

A GENERATIONAL CURSE

Once upon a time there was a little girl who new a old Lady who would have her sit down and tell her stories ooh my God Jesus these werent your every day stories that today people would tell or read to a child so the little old woman who began her journey telling stories as she would began by telling how life was like for herself as a very small little child and ooh yes living a different kind of life of poverty you see this old woman was brought up in a time of slavery and yes there were situations where the people in and of that time had to live up to the Authority and rules of what they called back then the slave master life was hard and ruff for those people

Back then and if for any reason they disobeyed the slave master my God how they were beaten unmercifully so the old woman told the little girl of how her parents would have to go out and chop the cotton in these very large cotton fields 'fields that went for miles and miles long one day the old woman told of how her parents left her and her twin siblings at home' yes indeed a place called a little shack of some sort but never the less it was home to them' so as the old woman and her too siblings sisters were home alone ooh my God the most horrific thing took place the slave masters kicked in and burst into the door in which terrible things had took

Place the old woman and too siblings would never forget such a horrible thing for the an Entire life time the slave master beat one twin sibling unmercifully and raped thee other twin sibling back then there were no Docters for the slaves like we go to now days so when the parents of all three siblings came back home they had to witness to this horrifying thing that had took place to these children while they were gone out in the fields chopping the cotton the father had took to pieces of wood shaved and took carved them into sticks from a tree limb branches

And stripped them of there leaves then smoothen the too sticks and made what we call today crutches that particular twin could not walk for six months because of what she had Endured from the slave master; as the mother had taken leaves from certain trees and plants and created a medication for pain ooh yes my God for they may not had an school education Back then but God made them wise to what to gather and make there medicine some of their Little shacks were miles apart from one another they walked for miles in the scorching heat some died because of the oldness of there ages it was unorthodox for them to speak of how they were treated but only amongst them selves some of the slaves were made to cook clean mop on there hands and knees the floors wash clothes some of the older ones were made to Breast

Feed the slave masters baby because the slave masters could not make or produce milk My God what a life for such a people but also God made them Strong and to this very day they are still strong because you see with God only the Strong Shall Survive Amen the true Kings and Queens are with in Gods hands cause he's the God that can give incomprehensible peace

But the Almighty God says that we may be Enduring for a Night but in the mourning Everythings gone be Alright' Amen yes prayer constantly is what made those people back then sustain such a horrible curse back then but we no that there is a God and he's a unconditional loving God all of the time and that the wages of Sin is indeed Death so when taking a life uncalled for that is truly a Sin in the Almighty Gods Eyes yet and still those people Survived some of them and

Still it is now a world of Prejudice but as long as the people keep Believeing in God in the Great Last Day all Tables shall be Turned and what once was the Tail Shall be the Head Amen and with that So Ends this short story of A Generational Curse if only Gods people would Commit and Believeth in his words his will and his way they shall have Ever Lasting Life from a Glorious fountain that will never run Dry Amen and that is why this Story was A Generational Curse

Burden Shall be Taken Away
ISAIAH 10:27

Year of 1978

A WOMAN WHO COMMITTED A SIN

Once upon a time there was a very young woman who God put a man into her life but the young woman was very foolish and ignorant to the fact that God placed this man into her life for healing of her sole, so the very young woman had an ex boy friend or so we call of todays world, the ex boy friend led the young woman to

Go out on a date with him sneacking behind the man back. God put in her life, and because the flesh is weak and greate temptation Is always placed before us the saved man sent from God would not give sex to the young woman so she told the ex boy friend ok I will go out with you, little did she no the unsaved ex boy friend

Was there straight from satan, so the ex boy friend took the young woman to a deserted trailer that a relative had past away in years ago the young woman said why or you taking me here I'am not comfortable here I feel a strange atmosphere here if thou something or some one is here with us, so the ex boy friend said it's just all in your mind nothing's here but me and you, when the ex-

Boy friend preceeded to perform sexual act upon the young woman she called out his name where are you it's so dark that I cant see you or feel you, the ex boy friend said to her I'am here see for your self feel me. So the young woman said ok I feel your lower body on me but I don't feel your upper body the ex boy friend said look I no you see me so the young woman looked, and she saw

The ex boy friend body suspended in mid air, it seem if thow he was not on her body at all so out of fear the young woman replied please take me home I don't like where we are I don't understand how are you on me when I see you in the air please stop, the young woman cried out take me home now, the ex boy friend replied to her okay I will take you back home right now. while dressing

Back into their clothing one can feel an evil presence in the old trailer in which the ex boy friend told the young woman she agreed, the ex boy friend be gain to mock the experience that took place in the old trailer by telling the young woman it seem like his spirit of the dead man was in there with them he also said to the young woman he probably was jealous and wish he could have.

You himself, the young woman replied please don't talk that way you are frightening me as they drove away in the car the young woman said I shouldn't had did what I done I feel bad I feel I've sinned I feel I've done something forbidden and it all had to take place in the dead man's old trailer I also feel like the Christian man I meet, that I have betrayed him if though I will be punished,

So the ex boy friend told the young woman he will never no. just us and God of coarse, so then getting the woman home. The young woman got out of the car and went into the house of her mother's feeling that feeling strongly that she could be punished for such a terrible sin that she let the temptation of the ex boy

Friend led her to do, while laying down on the bed the young woman said God forgive me before going to sleep, staring at the wall the woman's body began to feel lite and lifeless no energy whatsoever still staring at the wall the young woman eye's shute the young woman be gain to fall into this strange yet deep sleep.

All of a sudden the young woman's body began to floot off OF the bed into mid air the young woman had a very thin night glown on. that when she went to bed she still had the very clothes, she came home on, wind began to blow throughout the room paper knife's plate's all of such began to blow flying across the young woman and the room, but never hitting her, then all of a sudden this dark shadow image in the form of a file cabinet drawers stood over the young woman, so the young woman cried out put me down please, then all of a sudden the young woman cried out again Oh God please put me down then the dark shadow in the form of file cabinet dware's said to the young woman look at it, IT being a very small white lite that the bigger the small white

Lite got the brighter the room was, the lite was so glorifyingly bright and beautiful that the young woman said I can't look at it, it hurts my eye's to look at it, the dark shadow said to the young woman it's the one that's doing this to you the young woman screamed out again O God please make it stop please put me down, so the light said to the dark shadow put her down and go away.

Then all of a sudden the young woman's body came back down on to the bed the dark shadow in the form of a fileing cabinet dwares disappeared things stop flying in the room the wind stop blowing last the great and powerful glorious light from God himself went away, while the young woman was still laying there on the bed the lord spoke unto her saying whatever you do don't try to get up right away wait a while to give your body back it's full strength so the young woman obeyed the words of the lord when she did get up she was terribly weak her limbs and her body there was nombness throughout her entire body, so then as the young woman sat on the edge of the bed the lord told her stand up.

Slowly get your pillow and go into the next room where your mother is laying, for no reason what so ever go to the bath room and look at your self in the mirror for this is something you do not want to see. the young woman said God what happened to me so again the young woman obeyed God's word and layed on the other sofa in her mother's living room, the young woman mother suffering from emfazema of the lung, having a very bad cough on many occasion's as the young woman began to fall into another deep sleep this time but feeling cleansed in some way her mother began to cough this tormenting cough as cause her mother to total awakness of her sleep

The young woman's mother told of her the next morning that some thing tragic took place last night, the woman replied what mother what do you mean her mother told her I'd rather not talk of it but what ever happened you no that I'am not a Christian but last night made me your mother a quick believer in God so with curiosity the woman said please mother tell me what happen so her mother said if you insist last night I began to cough the cough I cough when it's out of control and need water to calm it, I wook up and noticed you were there laying on the other sofa in the living room, when I saw you Donna I did not see you instead I saw death, I saw a dead person laying on the other sofa your

Face had the face death. in other words you looked dead you were laying on your back and your hand's cross like a person in a casket, Donna that put so much fear in me that I said O God what's wrong with my daughter you no I don't even read the bible but that night I went and found a bible in the house and began to pray I

your mother prayed over you first daughter and then I went all through the house and prayed for my other children, and as your mother all I no is what ever happen last night God was truly with you and I the young woman say this to you who are reading this true story that when we sin we pay a price but with God's loving hands on us satan cannot achieve.

Ms Donna L Howard

THIS YOUNG WOMAN WAS ME AND I SAY UNTO YOU O LORD THANK YOU ONCE AGAIN THAT YOU JESUS FOR THE SPARROW THAT WATCHET OVER ME THAT NIGHT.

THE LORD IS MY ROCK
PSALMS 18:2

YEAR OF 1981

AN EPIC TRUE STORY

A SPIRIT DWELL'S IN THAT HOUSE

Once upon a time there was a very young woman who moved into a house built of brick walls of a project low income houseing the young woman had a five year old child at the time, after the first month in the house the neighbors would come and visit the young woman asking her was she a witch, the very young woman said

Or replied to the neighbors why do you say am I a witch the neighbors, said because every time someone moved into the house they die just like the old man that use to live in the house. the young woman said tell me about it I don't understand I'am just a young mother trying to make it with a small child. so the neighbors,

told to her of a very old hispanic man that was I'll to the point in which he soon was going to die but at the same time this Old hispanic man was very cruel angry bitter meaning just plain evil ways, that he carried within himself.

he was so stuberen that he told doctors, family members, and neighbors, that before

He be hospitalized that he would stay in his house until he dies, in his house, and so the old man took that sick and until that's, exactly where his faith landed him, to had finally passed away in his own house the young woman said O my God I didn't no that or I would have not moved in. the neighbors said there was a black

Family that moved in and they had a beautiful twelve year old daughter and at one time the twelve year old girl began to become sick strangely her illness was exactly like the old man's, and that eventually the girl died just like the old man which the same illness doctors could not understand but the girl died in

The house the same way the old man did to this day her parent's are confused about the girl's death and the strange things that happened in that house. after that neighbors told the young woman next a woman of about twenty five or twenty seven year's old moved into the house and she often told the neighbors of how

Strange things happened in that house after living there only six months she could not take it any more. the strange events and things happening, also that she was ran over by a car and remained on crutche's to the point of her leaving the house because with out proper use of her legs this twenty five or twenty seven year-

Old woman believed that she was going to die, so the young woman with the five year old child said I will pray over the house and ask God to protect me and my five year old child. so a year had went by once again, the neighbors came to the very young woman and said there is something strange about you for some reason we

Fill that you have some sort of power. that you can live in the house and not be harmed or your child, the neighbors replied to her what is it this power you have or why is it special that you have to not get hurt or harmed. the young woman said I just believe in

The holy blood of Jesus Christ and that is all I dwell on, is his holy blood and the powers Jesus have to save me, so the neighbors took her word for it and said we want to be as close to God and the blood of Jesus like you tell us what to do. so the young woman said just believe and he will save you from all evil, but

Little did the neighbors no that there was indeed something strange, going on in the house, for example when the young woman would come home there was allway's a shadow in the form of a man in the livingroom window, the young woman saw this on many occasions to the point in which she did not want to go into the house, when coming, into the house the young woman could see no one or nothing

Strange sounds performed in the house such as a bell, a church type bell from back in aged day's would rang this enormous church sounding bell would start to rang from the time on the clock of at mid night and continue to rang until one oclock at night this hearing of the ringing bells became very annoying and hard for the

Young woman to sleep, also causing the young woman to began to drink beer in order to fall asleep to not have to hear the bells and wondering if her child also hear the ringing sounds of the bells so one lazy summer night about nine oclock pm. the young woman ran herself bath water as she went back into the bathroom

To turn the running tub water off she could see a floating spirit in the tub the floating spirit appeared like white smoke except with facial feature's and arms also of white smoke that seem to float or gluide around in the tub, the young woman said to herself God I'am going to ignore that floating spirit in the tub and take

My bath. when the young woman got out of the tub from taking the the bath she sat down and preceeded to watch a movie on her TV. set when all of a sudden a very cold chile went across the young woman's shoulder's, which caused her to tremble from the chile, then the same cold chile went across her feet but this time she

Could see the floating spirit as it crossed past her feet, so once again she shook and trembled from such a cold freezer like Chile, so the young woman said again this time out loud the Blood of Jesus be with me. then all of a sudden the young woman had a radio in her kitchen the radio began to come on, volume at

It's full capacity. so the young woman turned the radio off by switching the nob off and went back and sat down. then all of a sudden the bathroom sink came on water running full blast, so she got up and turned it off went back and sat down. again this time the radio turned back on full volume at it's highest capacity so

The young woman unplugged the radio from the wall went back and sat down, but the water came back on in the bathroom from the bath room sink facet, so this time the young woman said who ever you are or what ever you are I'am not afraid of you I will turn this sink off for the last time and I mean for it to not come on anymore.

So the water didn't come on anymore but while going back to sit in the living room the radio came on at it's fullness of volume, the young woman frustrated and angry at this time said I'am not going to play with you any more I will not turn this radio off again. when she noticed that the cord from the radio was

Swinging hanging unplugged from the wall that's when she began to pray, and said O Lord God please protect me and my child I no that I'am not crazy but things are happening that's not normal, so she with the holy blood of Jesus Christ said again protect me and my child. so the young woman began to take the holy bible and

And walk around every room and wall she walked alone the inside of the house letting the holy bible touch the walls as she cried out the holy blood of Jesus Christ take this spirit Lord God away and to leave me and my child at peace, so that night when the young woman preceeded to go to bed at the stroke of midnight the

Rang of the loud bells began to start this time water seem to be running in the kitchen, pot's and pan's rambleing, kitchen cabinets, slamming, so the young woman got up to see who or what seem to be making all this noise in the kitchen when she saw nothing. No water running, no cabinet door's, opening no pots, are pan's,

Had been removed, so going back to her room as she go's into the childs room she put the small child in the bed with her she tooked, the bible and prayed O Lord God please show me a sign Lord to let me no that I'am not crazy. so that next morning getting the child ready for kindergarten school as the young woman walks a

Block walk and put the child on the kindergarten bus, and greeted the good by, moma love's you, when she walks back at twelve noon to meet the child on the school bus, as the young woman and the child walked back to the house, when opening the door the young woman said to the child did you have fun at school today the

Child replied yes moma, so the young woman said let's change your school clothe's and I will give you a snack before dinner the child replied ok moma while in the closet hanging up the childs clothing the child laying on the bed told the young woman pulling one sock off his little feet with the look of fear yet confused

Said moma don't you hear them bells ringing in the night?...
now when were faithful to God and we asketh of something
from the heart God allways answers our prayer's. so the
young woman with her back turn to the child began to cry,
hanging up the childs clothe's. and then it hit her as she
remembered that she had asked,

God to give her a sign to let her no that she's not crazy, so the
child waiting for an answer asked the young woman again
moma don't you hear them bells ringing in the night?...so
the young woman said I don't no but let's not talk about it
but God no's and that's all that matter then the child said
but why are you crying

Moma and the young woman said because I'am happy
that today I found something out, but you are to little to
understand but God showed me through you. I love you said
the young woman to the innocent small child. so then that
particular weekend the neighbor, being of hispanic woman
asked the young woman to baby sit

Her five children as her and her husband went out to
celebrate their anniversary, so for company of the five year
old child the young woman had she said yes I will baby sit
the children. So
About eleven o clock pm. that night the children were
all asleep the young woman's child was in his room, but
something told the

Young woman to go and check on the children before she
goe's to sleep when she did she found that two of the children
layed together on one end of the coach and the other two

layed down the opposite end of the coach but the two year old stood laying across his sister's and brother's also asleep. before the young woman

Could pick him up the two year old and lay him on the other sofa the young woman's five year old said moma can I go with you to check on them to, and she replied what's the matter you can't sleep either and he said no moma I can't sleep. so as the five year old reached out to hold his moma's hand and they held hands

Together they both walked into the living room and the five year old moma said to him look how much they love each other for they went to sleep all on the same coach together just like you and me haa moma the young woman replied yes just like you and me. But as the young woman and her child stood there all of a sudden the

Coach began to rise off the floor suspended in mid air but even strangely when the coach got half way towards the celling the five year old child yeld look moma, and the young woman cried out I see, I see, holding the child's hand tightly the young woman screamed telling the five year old child to keep quiet the child

Replied ok moma. as they both watched the children on the coach floated all the way to the celling of that house leaving five inch's from touching their little nose's, the young woman wanted to scream more and rush up to the children and say put them down but low and behold God was in the mist. God spoke to the young

Woman telling her don't, what ever you do don't go up to the children, don't be afraid it only want's you to see what it can do so the young woman obeying God's word to her, she began to cry tears falling from her face as she listen to God, her and her five year old child watching these children suspended in mid air

Then the coach was brought down slowly, as the young woman was praying deeply inside and as the tears fell from her face, then the young woman's child said to her moma did you see that the kids, were in the air she replied to the small child yes I saw it. Tonight you will sleep with moma just like there together and we

Will sleep with the holy bible under our pillows, and moma will pray to God please lord let nothing else happen to those children this night and that they don't remember of it. when there parents come to get them in the morning, and by the grace of God that morning the children seem to not indeed have no memory of what

Had took place involving them on that coach that night. and so the young woman said praise be to God for that, then the next night early about seven O Clock another evening the young woman's child said to her moma can I brush my teeth the young woman replied yes you can, while in the bathroom with both the child's

Knee's on the sink one hand balancing his little body and the other hand brushing his teeth the young woman was watching TV. when she realized that the child had been in the restroom at least an hole hour when she called out to the small child saying Baby you have been in that bathroom long enough you need to come

Out now and come watch TV. with moma but the child wouldn't answer, so she got up to go to the bathroom as she passed the child in the restroom with knee's on the edge of the sink both hands and arms hanging down by his side's, the young woman walked up to the child and said baby you must get down now, but the child just

Gazeing if thow he was in some sort of trans or hiptmotized in some way into the mirror. strangely his little body not falling off the sink the child seem to be of a statue with his little eye's never blinking, so the very young woman began to cry wanting so bad to touch or even remove the child, but out of fear because

she did not no what would happen if she made an attempt to do so. so she went back into the living room and preceeded to pray to God saying lord God what is wrong with my child and why won't he answer me. even after two more hours had went by the young woman noticed that the child still had not came out the bath

Room so being so afraid at ten O Clock the young woman took the bible to her bed room put it under her pillow, then all of a sudden God spoke to the young woman again to comfort her by saying Don't touch the child don't indeed try to remove the child it won't do you any good right now but go ahead to sleep and keep faith in

Your heart that the child will be allright, so the following morning about seven O Clock same time in which the child had went into that bathroom that night, the young woman came out of her bedroom as she began to pass the bathroom noticing that her young child was climbing down from the bathroom sink, so she replied to

The child are you just now coming out of the bathroom??? the young child with not a clue in the world of his being there all that night said so innocently yes moma you told me I can brush my teeth. so since she realized that the child seem to had no memory of what happened to him that night, so the lord said to the young

Woman don't fret yet don't speak of the incident that took place to the child last night that it would only confuse and frighten him. so again she obeyed God. Another weekend the young woman's sister needed a place to stay she was out on the streets and had no where to go so when arriving at the young woman's

House that she stayed in the sister said please let me stay I have no where else to go, so the young woman knowing of the strange, things going on in that house but hopeing her sister can handle, what she was about to experience told her OK. I can not put my sister out I love you to much, so the young woman offered her

Small child's room to her sister sometime's the small child still slept in the same room with his aunt, days began to go by and the sister said to the young woman the house is strange I can't explain it but I do no this much there is something

about the child's room it is earry and uncomfortable to sleep
in shadow's

And TV. squarelike image's perform in the room at nights
how do the child sleep in the room is totally beyond me,
what is it she replied to the young woman, the young woman
said I don't know all I do no is that I allways called on the
blood of Jesus and I pray that me and the child would be
allright living here, sometimes

When me and the child go to bed in my room a small bright
white light the size of a golf ball appears from the hallway,
and this light come's into the room with me and the child
and it seem's to allways focus around me and the child, the
child often reache's out to the little bright shinning light and
say's to the young

Woman look moma it is our friend. every night the light
come's to play with us then it stays with us and eventually
go's under the bed. with us on the bed the young woman
looks under the bed with the small child and see that it is
allways there this little light to this very day I believe that,
that light was the light of God,

And Jesus, the holy blood of Jesus had his shinning light
on me and the child all alone. the young woman's sister
eventually left saying she could not take the strange
atmosphere and environment of the house and that she
would rather be homeless then to have to stay in a house like
that. the young woman's sister only stayed,

three months, but the three months she was there was so comforting to the young woman, but then that Saturday weekend the young woman's mother arrived about eight O Clock in the morning knocking on the door, the young woman went to the door and said Mother what brings you hear so early in the morning, the young

Woman's mother said to her something's wrong something's going on but I don't no what it is the young woman said what do you mean mother, her mother said all last night I could not sleep and something told me first thing in the morning, for worrying about you and the child to go get you and the child out of the house

Before something bad happen to you or the child, and I say this to you who are reading this story the young woman never told her mother of the incidents that was taking place in that house, but low and behold God is a good God, for some how he lead her mother to no that something was indeed wrong, so with fear installed in

To the young woman she obeyed the fact that this was the work of God, so she told her mother OK, mother me and the child will go with you and as they began to pack strange things began to happen while in the closet things began to tumble and fall about to strike the young woman in the head. but with her mother being

Right there by her side, her mother was able to worn her to move out the way before anything could harm her. it just goe's to show you God is so loving and kind with his graciousness, he pooreth all over us, for he sent his loving caring angel's to protect and watch over this young woman and her small child, and all because

She believeth in the holy blood of Jesus Christ this woman was me Thank you Lord for sending those angel's to protect me and my child.

PRAISE BE TO GOD AND THAT SPECTACULAR SHINNING LIGHT. AMEN

> A SMALL WHITE PIERCING LIGHT WOULD COME FROM THE HALL AREA OF THAT HOUSE, AND WOULD ALLWAYS STAY UNDER THE BED, I BELIEVE THAT, THAT LIGHT WAS THE LIGHT OF JESUS.

HE SHALL SUSTAIN THEE
PSALMS 55:22

YEAR OF 1982

AN EPIC TRUE STORY

A MAN CARRY'S THE MARK OF THE BEAST

ONCE UPON a time there was a young woman who asked God to bring a good man into her life, a good man a caring man a understanding man a loving man she lived alone her and her child of almost six years old, this strong need for a man became very annoying and uncomfortable for the young woman, one day as she was waking and

Still seeking this perfect man, a very large woman called out to her to come hear the young woman said to the very large woman what is it and why do you want me, the large woman told her because I have been watching you, you are not a happy person you are seeking a good man in your life but right now you are miserable

The young woman said to the very large woman how do you no this that indeed it was true, so the very large woman told the young woman why don't you come in and I could explain to you better, so the young woman was skeptical but at the same time she indeed wanted to no how this strange very large woman she had never

Seen before in her life until that day could no at lease that much about her, so as the young woman walked in she noticed that the very large woman sat at a table, at this time the young woman was nervous and confused so the young woman start to ask questions, who are you she said to the very large woman, why do you have

A glass round ball on your table, the very large woman said slow down you don't ask the question's I do so the young woman said I don't understand what do you mean by only you ask the question's so the very large woman told her I will answer your question's one at a time you see the reason for the ball on the table is because

It is what I call a crystal ball and the very large woman said to her I can see into the future with that ball and the very large woman told her that she also can read tarot cards that predict, one's future. so the young woman did not believe and preceeded, to laugh saying I don't believe that you can do that no one

Can predict someone's future but God so the very large woman told the young woman I will prove it to you that I can indeed so the young woman said to her prove it to me, so the very large woman said to the young woman sit down at the table across from me so that I can pick up your entire ora, so the very young woman did

Not knowing what was happening, but she did as the very large woman told her. the large woman said to the young woman I see in this ball that you are lonely and have been through a lot mainly wanting, a good man to manifest in your life, but hold on the large woman said to the young woman I see to men that's going to come

Into your life, the large woman said to her both men will have money and good job's but one man is white thee other man is black the large woman said to the young woman which man do you prefer because what you choose will be very important please choose in making the right decision for in the end there's a price to pay,

So the young woman so confused about the hole idea. this large woman could somehow predict these things, the young woman said I choose the black man because I've never been with a white man before as for as an relationship, so at this time the very large woman said to her I feel and think you should choose the white

Man. the young woman said but why the large woman said because the white man has a better job than the black man he own's his own business and have lots of money, if you choose the white man you will never have to seek no more for a good man in your life and you will allway's have money and be a happy woman. but if you

Choose the black man I see something wrong with the issue of choosing, the black man the young woman said tell me what do you see that's so wrong, I want to no tell me the young woman said to the large woman, the large woman said but you don't really want to no what I see, but the very large woman said to ease your conscious I

Will only say this much to you the large woman said when you meat the black man the relationship will start off beautiful and joyous, for you and him but in the end terrible things will start to happen. so the very young woman said to the large woman what do you mean will he beat me, the large woman said no strange things

Will start to happen in the relationship, wicked things, things that you never experienced before will surface in the relationship, things that will have you lost and confused very frightening, to you so indeed months went by then one day the young woman met a white man the white man really admired the

Young woman he had so much money that it was frightening to the young woman, the white man told her if you be with me what I have could be all yours and that he owned his own business, so after seeing the white man for about three months a black man also came into the young woman's life, but because of the fact he

Was black and she had never experience a real relationship with a white man she one day told the white man that she enjoyed meating, him and what he had to offer her, but her sole tells her to go her way and let him go his way it seem to really disappoint the white man and hurt his feeling's but he told the young woman you

Will probably never find another man that could make you as happy as me but at the same token, I will respect your feeling's and go so indeed he left and she never saw him again the blackman however had a good job true enough and some money but the young woman, cared within her a kind of spirit that was not out for the

Money but for true love from the heart of the man but she was so happy of the black man she met that she somehow forget that the very large woman said to her that in the end there's usually a price to pay for the work and predictions's that she can do so the relationship was so perfect that one beautiful summer time of

The year she asked the black man's parent's or so she told them that she wanted to marry there son, the black man had parent's of a preacher serving God the black man's parent's were thrilled that the fact she the young woman wanted to marry their son now

I say this to you who are reading this story when were prosperous and happy in life, satan will intervene and try to stop what God has placed to be. so one lazy other day mid in the summer day, another black man came into the young woman's life and all because the first black man told the young woman that he felt she was moving to fast and that he was not yet ready for marriage to give

It there relationship just a little more time, so this hurted the young woman's feelings and she felt that in some horrible way she had been let down, back to the other blackman she met he had no parent's of God he drink the fire of the devil's water liquor but once again she was so hurt that she let herself become a weak

Tool for the other black man who solely seem to just serve the devil, this other black man began to come over the young woman's house but with the look of a young man and ways yet he was a very old man he was sixty five years of age and preceeded to tell the young woman because he wouldn't marry you I could

Make you happy be with me and you'll will see. but the young woman so easily leaded that indeed she fell into one of the devil's traps and all of a sudden jealousy formed in the relationship, one night the woman while laying in a bed together told the old black man she said to him I love you so much and I mean it from

My heart, the old man stated to her I no because I can see straight through your heart, with her head laying down on the old mans, chest. the young woman thought the words to came straight from her heart so beautiful, so she preceeded to look up at him the older black man in the face and noticed that it appeared he had

No eye's in his head at all but in stead eye's filled of blood and darkness this image of the older black man frieghten the young woman and she preceeded to scream out and cover her eye's saying to him O my God what is wrong with you, you must tell me your eye's they are not normal please go look at yourself in the

Mirror you will see what I'am talking about. so the older black man said to please you I will go and look at my self in your bath room mirror and with covering his eye's and face with his hands he came out and told her see there's nothing wrong with me I'am Ok now clam yourself down, so the young woman asked him to please

Leave and come back another time that she needed to be alone and try to understand what she saw that took place in her bedroom that night, so he said I understand I will go he also said that he meant no harm to scair are frieghten her for to please try and Understand. Another afternoon approached and because of the very

Spaced age difference between the young woman and the much older black man the relationship seem to loose it's fire and happiness the older black man became dull lifeless and just plain boring to the young and because she was not married to him she preceeded to go out one night she felt she had taking all she could of this

Lifeless unGodly person. so coming home late that night, the old man had stayed up and didn't go to sleep for no reason at all, as she unlocked the door of her house and preceeded to walk in the old man sat at the door in a lounge chair near the front door he preceeded asking her where she had been she smiled and said

Wouldn't you like to no, but he stated to her I do no where you have been you see you forget I have eye's in the back of my head and I can see you, where ever you go, who your with, also what you do, so the young woman preceede to laugh telling him that's crazy no one has eye's in the back of there head. the young woman

Said to him to avoid this foolish conversation I'am going to go to bed on you and because you are in my house I don't want to hear another word about me tonight, and most of all people with eye's in the back of their heads. so while laying on the sofa caoch the the young woman noticed that the much older man had become very

Silently still and quiet so she called out to him and he would not answer, so she looked up behind her shoulder and noticed that he sat in a manner in the lounge chair if thow to jump and attack as she looked at him she noticed his eye's were not of human all she could see was dark blackness of blood through out his entire

Eye's so she screamed and called out to him once again saying O my God what's wrong with you, your eye's don't look normal they don't even look human, in return he said to her turning his head slowly if thow he could hardly even move his head with a tone of voice of satan himself saying there's nothing wrong with me,

There's something wrong with you, the young woman replied to him no there isn't something wrong with me please go look for your self and you will see what I'am talking about, so as she stood in her kitchen behind the counter trembling so affraid but all the time calling on the blood of Jesus as her protecter. the older

Man said to her do you really want me to go see my self in the mirror, she replied yes please you are scaring me as she pleaded and begged he finally got up to see himself, while in the restroom the young woman ran to her bedroom locked the door got into her bed shaking trembling crying and with the bible she began to

Pray as she prayed these were her words she said father God and the holy blood of Jesus if he no's what he's doing to me send me a sign someone Will come to my house right now, and if he doesn't no what he looks like and this is not his doing then no one will come, God is a merciful and gracious God, for he answered the

The young woman's plea. by indeed sending someone to her house when were sincere from the heart God act's fast moment's after praying that pray the young woman's door bell rang, with altomate surprise the young woman jumped as her heart pumped very fast but God spoke to her saying do not no longer be affraide for

You asked me to give you a sign and I answered to your crying plea for I your God no's that your heart is sincere, so the young woman said to her self O yeah that's right I did ask for a sign. She began to cry for seeing the mercy of God is not only there for us but swift, she replied thank you lord O my God, thank you O God you are so fast because you love me that much. as the door

Bell kept ringing in a persistantly manner the old man said to her somebody's at your door do you want me to answer the door. Words dragging from his mouth still with the voice of satan himself, at first the young woman said nothing to him but when he screamed at her saying go ahead and answer the door, well you no God works in

Masterious ways it was the young woman's sister, O how God can put the joy back in one's heart, so the old man said it is your sister do you want me to let her in. the young woman said yes please let her in, he said with the voice of satan I cant hear you But God told the young woman to yell out so that satan no's

You don't no longer fear him, so as she yelled out obeying God's command the older man flead away from the door saying OK I will let her in the young woman's sister came directly to the bedroom door knocked and called out sister are you ok what's the matter with you is every thing allright open the door it's me your sister

The lord told the young woman get up and open the door for I have brought your sister to you. you have nothing to fear any more talk with your sister for I have sent her to comfort you in time of need. obeying God again she open the bedroom door as she was crying her sister said tell me what's wrong did the old man

Hurt you, you no that what ever it is I'am your sister and you can tell me. you no I was at home and something told me to go to your sister's house she needs you and I didn't really want to come out this late at night three o clock in the morning but some thing told me to go to your sister, now I'am hear tell me what's

Wrong remember something leaded me to come. so because blood is thick between to sister's she began to tell her sister, she said I came home late he told me he had eye's in the back of his head then his eye's sister were dark with the color of blood in them he did not even look human please sister tell me I'am not crazy

I have never seen such a thing like that in my life what is it what's wrong with him, the sister said to the young woman I will tell you, but you have to promise me that you will calm down, so the young woman agreed she would calm down her sister told her first of all by I'am hear he cant or wont hurt you he did what he

Did what he did to scair you because you laughed at him those are demon's in him and when there angry they take surface in the individual the young woman said but how do you no this sister O my God, how do you my sister no this. because I have experienced the same thing in a man I use to no when ever he beat me or was

Angry his eye's would turn, eye's of a demon. satan himself, but what did you do sister, I would just leave and when I came back home he was back normal. at first it use to scair me but God kept me stroung enoughf to deal with it until finally the relationship was over. you see sister when we come into things like this we

Must not let fear take place just call on God and he will be there to protect us also I must tell you that he know's that we are talking about him he know's exactly what we are saying he no's, what were going to do so for your sake, I say to you my sister let's just go and not talk about it anymore. I will also say this

To you he cant help the way he is he was born that way it is not something he asked for he is one of other's that was choosen to be what he is, one of satan's followers. but the good side of him had to care some what because if he had let you see him in the light you may have had a heart attack from the horror you would

Have seen as well as other horrible thing's could have happened, but like you said sister telling me the fear you had was so stroung that God stepped in and intervene for your sake. you sister God love's us and when we don't understand something he come's to comfort us I

Love my sister don't cry any more be stroung for God sent me to you. now to those of you who are reading this story never let man try to tell you that there is something awaiting for you, and that only God predict's, the true future for all of us and because the young

Woman didn't no any better she was blind to the act's of this very large woman, she experienced something that showed her that God is the true predictor of all things. this woman was me Jesus thank you for showing me truth from lie's and deseatfulness.

FOR I GIVE YOU THE PRAISE, THE GLORY, THE MERCY, THE HONOR, FOREVER, AMEN...

This older man had three six'es in the top of his head three six digit's that represents the sign, the mark of the beast. when combing through the sixty five year old man head the young woman replied to him wow. There are three six'es, digit like six'es that seem to

Be carved into the top right side of your head, the man's head appeared to not have a form of skin as a sculp but three six'es carved into the skull of his head he in return said what you see I was born this way and that with his eye's being the way they are he

Can see the dead the young woman replied but how, so he said I will exsplaine it to you. you see I can see spirits good one's or bad one's from the dead you see I was born different from you and most people I can talk to these spirit's they will tell me things if Iam

Willing to take the time to listen to them they tell me how they died why they died or how they died the old, man told the young woman He really don't no why he was born this way but as a child he said he hated hims self because of the strange way from normal people he was so he just learned to just live with it. that his mother said there's nothing that can be done about the way he is???????

A Man Carries The Mark of the Beast
Let There Be no Strife

Genesis 13:8

Ide Like to give A Special Praise and Thanks To The Lord
For The Story Written About The Man Carries The Mark
of the Beast; That Story God Indeed Brought That Man
Forward to let all of the World No That such A Person
Does Exist

Lord I Magnify Your Holy Precious Name

Amen

2-19-85

A TORN FAMILY

Once upon a time there was a family that was so torn apart that every body seem to be and see only them selves especially when it came to helping one another you see clearly a family or any household that doesn't carry the Light of God in them will always have hardship pain and of course misery of all sorts of of kind we must all no and remember God is the key to all of our ups and downs in life but in order to achieve a more Bountiful standard in life we must all always come together as Jesus did with his Disciples as they were Recognized as one Family in God many things can take a bad turn in life if we don't practice loving one another as we love our seleves but then at the same time one truly have to no villagently how to love our selves God is

Love take a moment and think about how Great is his love for us Amen you see he doesn't see one or another as the best his unconditional loving weather were bad are good you can always have God if you can learn to love back share help give in time of need of others we must all learn to be Diligent as God an example is to take a stand when someone has fallen down hurting searching for love of the right kind Gods love that is because there can only be one kind of love and that is the love of God and he is the most thankful of us when we show him that we will not let our Material things control our lives in other words never putting our material thing

Above or anyone we no who does not have such a thing we must remember those things indeed will perish some day but our Lord and Savior will never perish even until the ends of time who are what is greater then Thee no one or nothing Amen to those of us who do sometimes theses things can cause striff jealousy and even hatred among us and of the ways of God we must learn the way of giving sharing loving and helping each other that is truly the way of our God Amen so remember our iniquities will never let us prosper so in order to prosper we must be indulgent to one anothers needs Amen again a grossly unfair behavior can only cost us a sadden but bitter life

Of Turmoil and we can Honestly all admit that 'that is something all don't want in our Lives But Yet and still This Family could not find that kind of peace within there lives for even truly noing Who God Jesus that is Was yes Because their hearts and soles were not of God and His Holy Commandments so with to no God is to find him in your hearts and souls keeping him in our minds will forever bring us peace and peace of mind in his holy will and way for us all

And so Ends this short tell of this Story of how there Once was a Torn Family who Couldn't see or feel the Holy Presence of God so ins the Moral of this Story is that his Mercy Love Kindness His Grace his Glory he is always there by our sides Till the End of Time and by his Grace we Shall overcome Praise be to God for he gave his Strips for us when he was placed on that old Rugged Cross so in the Last Days we pray that This Family shell seek the Pure guidance of God Amen

Lord we Praise your Holy Name Of Jesus

BE kind one To Another
Ephesians 4'32

Year of 1986

A CHILD POSSESSED

Once upon a time in years since the Beginning of time such unnatural things used to take place in a world that we live in to this very day things that are unseen of unreal in some cases unbarable to the necked eyes' but just like way back then in the Biblical days and even when Jesus walked this earth people would come across a strange unheard of citation are circumstances called possession in some people ooh my God how this was a real eye opener

For the people and or any person who ever came in contact with such a paranormal person or event these people who was stricken with these types of possession were of Denoting events such as telekinesis or clairvoyance that are beyond the scope of normal scientific understanding for example there were children adults and even babys but to witness anyone like this can really make one Believe and no that there is a God such as Jesus Christ himself who can clearly heal protect and remove any infirmities from us all including casting out all that is not of

Righteousness and Holyness type or types of possessions you see God is of truth and only truth can restore what can be born into the world of pureness so in other words God can heal and remove such and all impurities from any one because he is the most highly and awesome creater there is so therefore we Thrive and Strive on his magnificent Greatness cause he indeed is our Ultimate Healer of all Things and for us to always remember God has not put the spirit of fear in us but the Spirit of Love Kindness and a Sound Mind and the Power of Love to

Seek out his Mighty Diligence we must continue to keep on Praying and Believing in him for he is the one who calls all the final shots and predicting judgement of us all and that is why its so important to seek out any and all repentance of the Sins of the world you see God didn't Create us to live a life of Sin but a of Forever Endurance of his loving Grace to live of all his commandments meaning the Truth the Life and the Way of him so when we seek out for the true ways of God nothing can Distort us from being True believers of God not even Things

Are people that have been made of possessed images so we can Proudly say with aloud praise Amen Ooh how Magnificent is he Thee Almighty God in Heaven that no one or nothing shall out any type of Fear in none of us so with that being said God removed these Entities from those who had became stricken with the Disease of Possession and will continue to do so Tell the Ends of time and the True moral of this story is that God can make any of us Hole and

Free again for all and any imperfections Lord we Thank you in Jesus Mighty Name Amen and to always

Remember prayer is the key to all things in Christ Jesus again we say we Love You So let us all Rejoice in Gods work of significate Approval of his Mighty Works Amen Jesus Amen

Thank Father God for Coming to Save The Whole Wide World

Amen

PEACE BE UNTO ALL
1 SAMUEL 25:6

Year of 1988

AN EPIC TRUE STORY

A HOMELESS WOMAN

Once upon a time there was a homeless young woman who had relative family member's friends, and because all do to the fact that our flesh can be weak her mother out of some form of hatred had the young woman's only child taken away from her, the mother of the young woman told her on a regular basis that she could not

Stand the young woman because she looked just like her father, so the young woman was very confused and could not understand that how is it that one can just hate the first born of her children for no apparent reason at all, so when the mother of the young woman had this child taken from her, her first and only born

Child she became homeless none of thee other relative's seem to care eigher, the young woman slept in parks allies even in the backs of people backyards sometime's she even slept in the back of her own mother's backyard until the light of God would appear out of the sky which would awaken the young woman, as she would

Thank the lord by saying thank you lord they may never no that I was here. the one they put out onto the streets, neighbors began to talk saying you have a very cruel mother what kind of mother would have her first born, first born child taken away and yet seem to have no conscious or care in the world of where her daughter,

Might be or if she's even dead. the young woman said I don't no and I don't no why she seems to even hate me I did not ask to be born, these neighbors said to the young woman as they would tell her stand and wait in the allie as they would bring her food to feed her, one day you shall witness the day of your mother suffering,

And only you your name she shall call upon, the young woman just dropped her head and began her long journey of homelessness as dark approaches she began to make her bed in the park going to door to door asking different people please give her a blanket or throw away pillows something that they no longer seem to care

About, telling them you see I'am homeless please help me, so the different people had mercy just like Jesus did when the hungry, the blind, the lame, and the afflicted, with disease came to him in the biblical days, and so there hearts went out to the young homeless woman in every way that they could possibly help,

One quiet night as the young homeless woman made her bed unto the grass on the park ground there were four people who walked up to play basket ball in the park as they did the young woman laying there with her head on her bible noticed that tow of them were young boys and tow of them were young men, all of a sudden the

Young woman began to pray asking the lord to protect her and to let nothing bad ever happen to her as she prayed she also asked God to send an angel to protect and watch over her. late that night a big snow white shaggie dog appeared from no where this dog when the young woman opened her eye's was standing there the

Dog licking on her face, so with out realizing that God had indeed answered her sincere pray, the dog was sent by God to watch over and protect her, then another night as the young homeless woman made her bed in the park the same guy's that were in the park day's ago came back this time with mischief cruelty and

Sin in there hearts, for one of them said out loud look at her she await's us, every night she is allway's laying there in the park why he say's then one guy said O man she's probably hungry and homeless, so the other guy said no I no what she wants, she wants us man and she wants us bad. so I'am going over there to

Give her what she want. but low and behold the young woman cryed out to God and said lord God please don't let them harm me please don't let them rape me, trembling out of fear and shaking as tears fell from her eyes, when the one particular guy said I'am going over there and if she's sleep I'll wake her up when I get through

With her. the other guy's called out to him saying no man just leave her alone, leave it alone, foolit's not worth it, but instead he came on over the fence and as he got one leg over and thee other leg halfway allmost over, the big snow white shaggie dog sent by God to protect the young woman arouse and ran over to

The fence the dog put one of the young man's ankle in it's mouth and began to grawel letting him no that if he even make's an attempt to harm the young homeless woman he indeed would be in grade a mistaken other word in error, so the young man began to scream and plead and cry out saying to the snow white big dog let

Me go but the dog kept holding him hostage, then all of a sudden he cryed out to the young homeless woman saying please is it your dog, is it your dog finally the young homeless woman said he doesn't belong to me, he is not my dog, as the young man trembled in fear shaking and screaming for dear life, the young homeless

Woman said come hear boy to the dog very mild and kindly and the big white shaggie dog listened to her, and obeyed her command as the young man jumped down and ran for dear life, and all the fear the young homeless woman had in her left, for God stepped in and comforted her through that grate big snow white shaggie dog

The one sent by God as an angel and that's when the young homeless woman held the dog tightly and said God now I no for you sent me an angel through the grate big snow white shaggie dog holding on constantly tightly to the dog as she's saying thank you God thank you Jesus praise be to you God for sending my angel to protect me

The young homeless woman saw thing's she had never in her life saw before, women rape women beaten poor women and men on drugs shaking in corner's of allie's begging her to watch over them if thou she was some saint sent from God and she the young woman said why and they would reply because as I shoot this drug in me you must

Watch to see that I don't go to sleep for if I do then this means I have overdosed but the young homeless woman began to cry out as she begged please don't make me do this I don't no what to do. I never seen some one shoot their drug's, I'am no doctor if you should die, your making me feel like in some horrible way it was

My fault, so they would tell her but see your homeless just like us and if it were you I would watch your back so the young homeless woman said okay but I will turn my back I don't want to see something Ive never seen before and as she turned her back she began to pray she prayed a prayer asking of God in the holy name

Of God in heaven and the holy blood of Jesus in heaven please Lord God let not this poor homeless individual's sole be wasted from his or her body let not them go to hell because of a weakness, of one of satan's traps O lord God please hear my prayer. And as the young homeless woman turned back around she saw that

THE INDIVIDUAL INDEED GOD HAD WATCHED OVER HIS POOR SOUL AND I SAY THIS TO ALL WHO'S READING THIS STORY THROUGH IT ALL GOD ALL WAYS, HAD HIS WATCHING ANGEL'S EYE'S UPON THAT YOUNG HOMELESS WOMAN AND NO MATTER WHAT A MOTHER OR RELATIVE MAY DO TO US GOD ALLWAY'S TAKE CARE OF HIS OWN FOR HIS OWN WAS ME A HOMELESS CHILD OF GOD, I GIVE HIM PRAISE AND GLORY AND THANKS TO THIS VERY DAY THAT HIS ANGEL'S WERE PROTECTING ME ALL ALONE. YOU SEE FOR THIS YOUNG HOMELESS WOMAN WAS ME

IN JESUS PRECIOUS NAME AMEN.

HOW GREAT IS HIS GOODNESS
ZECHARIAH 9:17

Year of 1989

AN EPIC TRUE STORY

A WOMAN GOD SPOKE TO

There once was a woman and she lived in poverty. trying so hard to make it, but whoo-low and behold god was allway's by her side, this woman had family member's who seem to just never care. And no matter trouble or help she was in these family member's were Never their when she struggled to have money, a home, food, or

Clothing, these family member's came to her yet but with the little, she had for God touched her heart and sole with so much love and care that she gave and even thow it left her with nothing much. God so loved his only begotten son that who so ever belie-Veth, in him shall have charities of the world. when this woman

Came totally to God and bowed down on her hand's and knee's he showed her the light and he came to her, Hallelujah when she asked of him deer Lord what can I do to make things better in relationship, family, children, and my brother's, and sister's, of God he answered to her in her sleep one night be stroung, be

Stroung donna for you will make it in the end. For God truly

Bless the child who has his own in Jesus name I praise you.

THE LORD SPOKE TO ME ONE AFTER BAPTISM ON A EASTER SUNDAY IN THE YEAR OF 1989 I SHALL NEVER FOR GET HIS STROUNG, YET FRIGHTENING, YET BEAUTIFUL, VOICE OF THE LORD....

BE THANKFUL UNTO HIM AND BLESS HIS NAME

PSALMS 100:4

Year of 1990

AN EPIC TRUE STORY

A WOMAN'S TRUE MAN IN GOD

There once was a man in one's life, I really looked up to the fact that he was a man and he said things that made me fell so free, as well as he let me no that I was a woman. but in these seventeen year's I come to a time and point of one's life to realize that he was only using the special beautiful gift's that

God had provided me with, so there came that particular day that I saw the glorifying light, and I woke up. one new then that this special one was put here to do God's deed's and god's will in other words, a woman was not put on earth to be disrespected, abused, or put down, for a woman this particular one was meant

To be treated with all the GLORY, LOVE, JOY, HAPPINESS, STRENGTH, GUILDDENCE, SECURITY, WARMTH, COMFORT, SUPPORT, ENTHUSIASM, YET with the most uplifting, self-Asteam, for this one this woman that is me. and God created me as a peace giver and pleasure Receiver from that special man whom is God himself...

HALALUYA I LOVE YOU GOD MY MAN IN JESUS...

I HAVE PUT MY TRUST IN THE LORD
PSALMS 73:28

Year of 1992

AN EPIC TRUE STORY

A WOMAN WITH PENNY'S

There once was a female, this particular female had experienced a time in her life where it was time to make some thing of herself and that some thing had to be more than education, job, carrier, or money, then it came to her that the best way for her to find success in the world was to realize her successor, which is none other than God himself, for not only did she gain and obtain a job to better her survival in life she gained in her job working for God, the lord, he led this female to earn an education the job she was comfort with the carrier she prospered in. the money came bountifully she gained a home that she was top Queen of she gained a bank account, that said in her name with number's

Mutipully. most of all she gained knowledge that told herself that no one can make it if he or she doesn't put first God our Lord and savior first, for this Woman is me and that nothing's impossible as long as, God alone her side.

FOR I shall live a long prosperous life in God Jesus Christ and MONEY CAN ONLY BE WITH GOD's TOUCH AS A SURVIVAL.

THOU SHALT MAKE THY WAY PROSPEROUS
JOSHUA 1:8

February 14 2014

A WITNESSING FROM THE HOLY SPIRIT

Once upon a time there was a woman who witness things that in thee ordinary realm of things in Life we normally don't conceive or see but my god this woman witness things that she knew only God himself could have foretold to anyone because it was some what to her not natural in the living world that we live in there was a man who had declared himself as her fiance and promised to marry her some day but sadly he past away so the marriage never took place strange events began to take place and happening the first strange thing to take place was on the very night of him passing away and fire fighters parametric and coroners had removed his lifeless small little body crying and grieving so because of the lost of him she

Finally feel asleep and while sleeping it seems if tho he was sitting on a small stool beside the bed where she layed sleeping smiling watching her ass she slept because she could see him smiling in her sleep she awaken open her eyes and saw no one was there ooh yes this Dream seemed so real that she sat up in the bed and said out wordly I know you were here all the time as she was sleeping another strange thing took place when he was alive and would leave his key to get in the house he would tap the bedroom window to let her no he was back home and

Call out to her letting her no that it indeed him the second night of his passing away she heard a tapping sound on the bedroom window but when she looked out the window there was no one or nothing there so she sat back down on to the bed started to cry and say ooh my God that is the way he used to tap on the window now you who are reading this story stay with me as the third night of his passing away the lights in the bedroom lamps that is would began to go on and off but because she shared the love of God so deeply in her heart she did not let that Affect her in anyway as she knew the Holy Spirit was with her and so on the fourth night what strangely happened there was a bell he had given to her when he was still living alive that is and the bell had the words on it said you are so special to me I Love You well as she was lying in bed on that fourth night the bell was in the living room on a table and the bell began to ring but once

Again she knew that it wasn't normal for that to happen and keeping in mind that God was there with her she just ignored it and went back to sleep' stay with me people on the fifth night had another dream this dream to seemed ooh so real because when he was living he would always tell her when he was gone I never put anything on the stove and leave it cooking and Go back to bed ooh 'ooh'

ooh Glory be to God for this dream indeed was a Super Natural witnessing early that next mourning the woman had put a pot of stew on the stove turned the fire down low on the pot still mourning and grieving over the lost of her fiance she went back to bed as she went into a deep sleep she started dreaming again that her fiance had came home

Walked into the living room to bags in his hand of food he had called out to her and said honey I'm home in that very instant of her dreaming she could actually smell the food food cooking on The stove smelling the beautiful aroma of the food she open her eyes sat up in the bed and said outwardly ooh my God he told me to never go to bed with the food cooking on the stove

So she ran as fast as she can to the kitchen and witness a miracle that there were about an inch of water remaining in the pot and the food did not burn as she walked out of the kitchen sat down on the living room sofa putting both of her hands over her face cried out loud saying these words thank you God for not letting the food burn putting her hands down from her face

As she's looking at the middle of the living room floor and said thank you too fiance for waking me up because you had came home later some preachers of a couple of churches told the woman that reality her fiance wasn't really home but in the spiritual realm he did come to let her no to get up because God had chosen that to happen as a Super Natural Witnessing Amen there also was a six and final dream this dream indeed to on this day opened this woman's eyes to what may be reality spiritual and super natural and of course the living as she slept on

On the six night she began to go into another deep dream this time the fiance said To Her In the dream you see my love I can see you and I no that you are with that man but only in the dream it was true but in reality there was no man so she replied what do you mean there is no man then he told her yes there is the man is tall and bright complexion then he replied to her if you like this man then be with that man I want you to live you life and don't cry anymore

He said to her you see I have decided to be with the family I never was with for all these years this confused the woman but upon waking up from the dream she realized that his mother died as she gave birth to him and in all reality he was with that family of his life but another thing puzzled the woman and that was the fact that there never was any other man in her life so sitting up in the bed she cried out ooh God what man there is no man but ooh Glory be to God eight years and eight months later the woman indeed met a man of tall bright skin Structure this

Was the greatest thing that could have happen in her life you see this tall handsome man was A Godly man ooh yes he believed in God just like her and through out those lonely years here God brings a man to now make her a happy and joyful woman Amen yes won't he do it Thee Almighty God that is and so the Great Morality of this story is that God

Ms Donna L Howard

can Super Naturally let you Dream a Vision that seems so
real but only in A Spiritual Realm Amen

Thank You Jesus

For God is so Miraculous Works Amen Again

COMFORT YOUR HEARTS
Colossians 4:8

For God is so Miraculous in his Works Amen Again

Year of 2003

A FRIEND SATAN LEADED

This friend lived in a atmosphere and world of drugs when this other young woman tried to live by God will and God's way of life the friend came to her and lead her to astray, by offering to her the devil's drug this DRUG had such a stroung hold that the woman found herself

Weak and helpless she could not for some reason fight this attack, that the friend sent to her by the devil, so this poor woman found her self lost and without thing's such as clothing

Food and finally her home woman had a child the child was nine year's old at the time the friend that came to the woman had a home yet when the woman went to the friend to seek help the friend turned her back on the woman and child the woman

Was led by the landlord to get out or be put out by the law so the woman cried as she asked, o lord what's going to happen to me and this child, we have no where to go so the woman walked the street's, with as many bag's that she could carry with homeless Child, from out of nowhere another woman portraying to be

Of God took the woman and child in when on the third day this woman to betrayed the poor woman and child by throwing them out back unto the street's, of poverty but low and behold God gave to the poor woman a job the job kept the woman and child in a motel from one payday to the next but once again the woman because of

The area and life style of the people around her, drugs in every direction she looked upon the woman was led to fall again. one night the woman listened to the devil by paying only three day's Of her rent and the devil told her to go ahead and use the rest of The money on the drug's the woman was under an influence for

Three day's of drugs the third night when there was no more drugs the woman had to make a decision it was either take what's left and by food for the child or try to pay another day or to for rent all that night this woman could not- sleep she tossed and turn and cried and began to beg God, saying help me I don't no what to do

Even thow, she had a mother and relatives but she new she could not strust them if she went for help. and by the graise of God this woman loved her child, so once again she cried out to the lord asking begging for his forgiveness, then God told her what to do. he said to her you must now pray and be very strounge no matter what

For your self as well as the child, for the child was in the next bed innocently sleeping not knowing what lies ahead in his or his mother's life, and as the woman obeyed God she cried out one last time this woman on her knees she crawled out of the bed and said faithfully to God. help me God help me I'am sorry I'am so sorry father

God help your child lord help me, father tell me.

So the lord told her the woman cry no more and be stroung for the sake of child

In the morning get your self ready for work and the lord said go to the work for the devil cannot have a chance to weaken you at work take the child to a Christian relative before going to work and that all you have to do is believe and keep faith and pray that things is going to be allright. I want the people of the world to no that who so ever shall call upon the name of the Lord God he is allways right there by your side and with a little bite of Faith, Prayer, believing in God God shall bring you through. just like he did for me.

In Jesus Holy Name, O my father God I love you,
This woman was me. Praise be to GOD.

Good SHALL COME UNTO THEE

JOB 22:21

JANUARY OF 2004

AN EPIC TRUE STORY

A PROPHET OF GOD

Once upon a time a woman had a prophet sent to her from God, the prophet told the woman in a letter that the holy spirit was going to come to her and tell her where she stands in her life, well the night of the year January 5-2005 pm. late in the night the holy spirit came to her in a dream, the dream was so miraculously

Devine and spiritual that it felt to the woman like all had happened, to her the man in the woman's life at that time was also seeking God, so all of a sudden when the holy ghost appeared it appeared talking to the woman about her life and what she is to expect in her life, when suddenly the devil tried to not let her

Hear what the lord was telling her through her man about her life so the woman called out praise God then all of a sudden the womans,' soul was lifted from her body she saw a glorious atmosphere. And kept saying praise God, and also saying now I see Lord now I see then said as she kept praising God, then she was brought

Back down unto her bed. when the woman woke up from her sleep it was about 5:45 in the morning she told of her experience with God to her man and also told her man that God told her spirit that her man is special. that he has a holy annionting about himself and that he should seek more knowledge from God concerning

This holy annionting for God care's...
THIS WOMAN SAID PRAISE BE TO GOD FOR GIVING ME SUCH A PROPHET AND THAT I SHALL NEVER FORGET THAT BEAUTIFUL, HOLY, DEVINE, SPECIAL EVENT THAT TOOK PLACE IN HER LIFE THAT AWESOME NIGHT THIS WOMAN IS ME DONNA.

PRAISE BE TO GOD AMEN.

HIS UNDERSTANDING IS INFINITE
PSALMS 147:5

2-2005

AN EPIC TRUE STORY

A YOUNG WOMAN WHO FOUND JESUS

Once upon a time there was this young woman and after experiencing things that seem to just have no explanation at all; and going through life having ups' and downs' majorly in her life; after crying for help strength and guidance of the right kind she decided to finally give Jesus a try and woo; low and behold finding Jesus was indeed the greatest thing she could have ever done in her life; for nights when she was alone; days and nights when she was afraid and even when she had to take on task all by her self Jesus always seem to step in and be right there know what makes finding Jesus so wonderful is that he

Will make things alright in your life just like he did for me the young woman; you see Jesus He took the fear out of the young woman heart and provided means for her to stand up and make it on her own the proper way she found that when taking time out of your day to pray; that day becomes a perfect day; that no matter where you go or who you run into troublemakers from the past Jesus shields you from the enemy; and no matter what the enemy trys he cannot defeat the holy power of God Christ himself, know when this young woman found Jesus tremendous changes started happening in her life first of all Jesus cleanses your spirit and that

Makes you a Beautiful yet glowing appearance for some one's eyes to see relatives of the young woman saw the change old time worldly friends saw the miraculous change; all telling the young woman there is something different about you; you don't look the way you used to look what is it, please tell us so the young woman said with her heart filled with joy; ooh there's something totally different about me alright; you see I found Jesus; and all of the time when I was suffering and had been let down by most of you Jesus cared enough for me that he one day I said ooh lord I am tired of going through this

Rough and hard life there's got to be something better Lord then this. sickness, affraide, and most of all suffering YOUou see when I this young woman called out upon the name of Jesus he opened my eye's to the world and he showed me as well as he was guided me, he also showed me that this is the light

And the life you really want to see, for he also let me no that for each and every time I shead a tear that my tear's shall be captured and placed into a jar for the wonderful day when we all go down that golden stairway to heaven, and I say this me This young woman, there's nothing on God's green earth like

Finding Jesus, you no he restoreth my terrible soul. and cleansed and polished it, and made me today what I call hole, I'am glad that I found Jesus, and I shall tell of the world every day of my life that he gives me breath to breeth, that there is truly only One God and that God is Jesus. you see when I was scared he said

To me, Jesus said fear not for I have put the joyful screams of praises within you. your fear is now a thing of the past today your heart holds courage of joy, praise God. and when I thaught it was over Jesus showed me it was just beginning. and when I thaught I feld Jesus showed me opposite I had succeeded. when

I thaught I was lost he, Jesus showed me that I was found. when I thaught nobody cared Jesus showed me take not refuge in man but no that I am there, for Jesus told me he care's, when I thaught that I was going to die, JESUS from falling out of a moving vehicle of fifty mile's per hour Jesus came and he lifted me up off

Of the ground. when people said I was ugly Jesus said to me look open your eye's and see the beauty I have prone within you. when they laughed at me Jesus said to me the day will come when thee shall have ever lasting laughter. when they talked about me like a dirty dog Jesus said to me fret not for they are only talking

About them selve's.

When they lied on me Jesus, leadeth what was once in the dark revile and come to the light. when doctor's said it was all over for my mother and child Jesus, said to me believeth in me for I your lord God can indeed cure all. and it was that today my mother and child live's on. and this

Revelations from Jesus to a young Woman who found Jesus;

Is all because I found Jesus, When I thaught I was going to loose my mind Jesus, said to me now your mind is set free from all the eniquty's that you have suffered from. when they mocked me Jesus, said to me let not your heart be filled with sorrow for they shall wither away like the drying leave's

Off of a dead tree. I say this to you when you find Jesus all the missing peace's of your life forms together, for God is a good God, he's an awesome God and why we give thanks and praises and glory to him every day. for with out Jesus I would be lost and no way to turn but again I say I'am so glade that I indeed

Found Jesus, and that young woman who found Jesus is indeed Me.

O LORD GOD THANK YOU, I THANK YOU EVERY DAY ON BENDED KNEE'S FOR LETTING ME FIND JESUS. AMEN

THE JOY OF THE LORD IS YOUR STRENGTH
NEHEMIAH 8:10

3-2005

AN EPIC TRUE STORY

A WOMAN WHO LIVE'S FOR GOD

Once upon a time there was this young woman and you no what, a beautiful, sanctual, glorious, thing be gain to form in her Life every morning she would get up at the break of dawn and get on her knee's and just praise and pray to God. and as she started her journey of the day people said to her there is a heavenly

Glow about yourself what is this beautiful glow upon you and, the you young woman would say, Ohh it's just the glory of God for which I praise him every morning he puts breath into my body, now when living for God, doe's not just mean giving him praise's every morning but making sacrifices, such as fasting, for God.

Vow's for God. and most of all attending a holy ground church for God. all of these things combined made living for God a solid foundation for the young woman you see when were sincere with God God poors his blessings upon us, this young woman experience in her living for God blessings she thaught once upon a time could

Have never been, but God's loving grace and mercy, he showed the young woman all of the beautiful yet prosperous things she own as well as have all, because she live's for God, you see she was never without no matter what she kept money a home a car clothe's food and other esentual's God also placed within her

Heart to allway's remember her back ground and where she came from, you see she came from whince she had nothing and she learned the hard way that it doe'snt take money to live but the loveof God is what make's us live on. so as she prosperd, her heart often remembered her past and so she gave, to the homeless to the

Hungry to the poor to the needy she helped the the sick the weak the lame the deformed she gave money's to charity's ministry's shelter's people over in country's without a mean's of support and all of this because she live's for God. when they came and knocked, on her door and said they had no where to go she took them

In and said they had no where to go, when they came and knocked on her door and said they were hungrey she feed them when they came and knocked on her door and said they had nothing to wear no clothing she gave to them what clothing she could spear for God's love is so kind and gracious that she learned to hold the kind of

Love that God love's within her heart, now some of this people may have been people from her past that did her wrong and looked down upon her, but she still cared the love of God for them and helped in the best way that she could, and did you no for every time that her heart went out for someone God blessed her ten

Time fold for he is an awesome God and just living for God has brought so much joy and happiness in her life that not a day goe's by in which the young woman is not thrilled for the many surprising exciting miracle blessing's God place's before her life daily she is smiled upon, people tell her, stranger's that she

Has a very special annointing about her self and that she is indeed blessed, some even ask her to stop where ever she is to pray for them, to lay her holy anointing hands upon there body, praise God, they also ask her as she's praying for them to ask God to strengthen them and to make them hole like her in the body

Of Christ. this my friends in Christ, give's her the young woman greate joy for she noe's she is working in all the ways for God. and you no what I say this to all of you my beloved brothers and sisters in Christ that this young woman is me once again in

JESUS HOLY PRECIOUS NAME, LORD GOD I GIVE YOU THE THANK'S, PRAISE'S, AND THE GLORY, AMEN.

3-2005

IN EVERY THING YE ARE ENRICHED BY HIM

1st CORINTHIANS 1:5

4-2005

A WOMAN WHO LIVE'S FOR CHRIST

Once upon a time there was this young woman whom after finding Jesus in her life she decided to just go ahead and devote herself by simply just living for Christ, Christ or Lord, o my God what a glorious thing it is to just live for Christ, you see amazing thing's happen when you decide to live for Christ. every day

Seeks strength and guidence truth and honesty honoring our God Christ most of all just the love of Christ field this young woman's heart and sole with so much joy that she no's Christ power is fowfilled within her. If you ever sat down, and had a vision or a dream Christ fowfilled that vision and dream, for you just like

HE did for this young woman, know when I say that she live's for Christ, this is what Christ doe's for her, every morning the young woman wake's up to the sound of the birds telling her of His creative grace, is beautiful, everyday as she take her journey throughout the nation preaching and passing Christ holy words

To some lonely souls ears brings upon a smile upon her face, every night before going to sleep, and just praiseing, and thanking God for all he's done for her becomes a more bountiful blessed days ahead, every step that she takes as she seeks Christ closerness pulls her more and more, her heart string's closer to Christ, every

Time she eat's shes reminded that, that for every bite of food that is placed in her mouth Christ provided solely just for her. That the frute's of life shall be hers as she live's for Christ abunduntly, for she is also reminded that when she looks up to the sky's of heaven at night and watchet of the heavenly stars

That Christ or Lord came one night as a baby in a manger to shed His blood for us. O I say what a glorious God we have in Christ. And what a pleasure it is to serve Christ. and live for Christ, when she seeks a new job she no's that it is the awesome power of Christ that touche's the hearts and sole's to make that boss to

Give to her that new job, when she seek's to own not just one beautiful home but several home's, when she seek's to own not just one vehicle but several vehicle's, and all because she lives for Christ., I this young woman don't no what I would have done if I had not learned to live for Christ, but I do no this much Christ has indeed

Has taken me on a higher plaine a higher plaine of supernatural abundence and fowfilement for can't no man or nothing take you higher than Christ. when I'am feeling a little low or down, he place's me in what I call a spiritual realm this spiritual realm keeps me flowing above all that trys to keep me down,

Just living for Christ you see satan the devil has no win. when it come's to Christ for he is allway's there one step ahead of me when the enemy try to come near me, Iam allways reminded of how to be aware of false witnesses, for Christ love's me, when they approache's me in sheeps clothing, yet the smile of the devil him

Self. Christ reminds me to go the opposite direction and that Iam now maid of hole to fall for such deseatfulness, for Christ love's me. and when you live for Christ you are placed in a spirit that defeats the purpose of falseness. for it every day of my Life and the false runs he fleads away from me he hide's from me

For I am made of which hole by the holy body of Christ. for Christ has givin me the ability to pick up the spirit of the sinner, the wicked, the unjust, and when he see's the light of Christ that shines upon me he fleads awy for his unholy sole can't withstand such glory and holy ness coming down straight from the

Light of Christ. You see when destrote and elimate's of the unrightous come at me Christ has strengthen me with the will power to over come those unfaithful temptations, for Chirist he loves me, for when lonlyness, trouble, or just plaine serching, for a peace of mind, Christ come's from a far from out of the mist, to

Assure me that I may have been enduring for a night, but low, and behold every things going to be allright, you see again Christ love's me It has been an experience I will never forget, for the rest of my life how it all come to me to be that it was my destiny, to witness these phenomenal things, for you see I was a

Choosen one sent straight from heaven from the day I was born to the day I die, Perish. to live for Christ and to tell of all the world his Maraculous, Devine, Glory, for Christ stood by my side from the begining to the end this unexplainable life I had leaded, and as I serve to live for Christ I no in my heart and

Sole that, that awsom day shall come upon which I will no all of why I was a choosen one, for Christ he said to me that he would not put more than I can stand upon my heart, but that I will live and learn from these task and experiences, for Christ new ahead Of time that what I saught shell be spoken of, to many generations,

And many generations to come, I say to you again and again HE... Christ is an awsom God and the more I speak of him the more I feel his holy presence so near me sometimes I even feel like I can reach out and touch him, for Christ he love me and as I close this story I want to say to you who are reading this book that

Every thing I told you happened by God's will for this woman was me and now lets take the time to praise our God Christ o glory shoutout onto God Christ lets lift up his name our God Christ the Lord for he is the most high...

PRAISE GOD.

JESUS AS I COME BEFORE YOU ON BENDED KNEES
LET ME THANK THEE O LORD FOR LETTING ME
COME TO LIVE A LIFE FOR CHRIST.
THY WORK SHALL BE REWARDED

JEREMIAH 31:16

5-2005

A WOMAN WHO WORSHOP'S CHRIST

Once upon a time there was this transformed and beautiful woman who cared the light of Christ upon her self being. this woman was so maraculously field with the awesome anointing of Christ that she was driven from a devine apparell to solely worshop our God Christ. from the time she saught the glorious morning daylight to

The time she saught the quiet wisper's of the night she would began to praise our God Christ. and as she did she made it the rock and foundation of her day to just say on bended knee's lord God my Christ, my father, in heaven for I give unto you the thanks I give unto you the praises I give unto you the glory for I magnefy

Your holy precious name. and in doing so she notice that the holy Ghost would fill her sole, body, and mind, as her body would jump shake and tremble from the devine holy spirit. the very first time this happened the young woman was affraide the second time Christ reveal to her now that you no there's no need to be affraide but to only let your self withstand this holy anniounting

Devine presence from me your lord God Christ, praise be to God the young woman said out loud as she also said my father God who which art in heaven I finally no for sure that I'am completely maid of hole in your body and that my sole is completely cleansed of all terrible inniquty's from my past. for I no my God Christ that you and only you holds the key to my salvation, for I no

That you also no that, you my lord Christ created the very being of my presence that rest in your gracious loving merciful arms. The woman praises Christ again this time with a high jump in the thee air as she totally stomps on the devil as she laughs at the devil saying to the pits of hell you are and there you will stay. In the name of Jesus and the holy blood of Jesus Christ. For

Christ is my master and I will always be my master's servant for I this woman serve's and worshops my God Christ, for he was my rock to stand upon through the highs and the lows in my life for He has let me really no who I am for he has shown me the gift that still's within me. as I serve him my lord Christ in measurements unknown the gift to speak out loud writing his devine holy

Miracles, and I also no that I'am indeed a writer but a writer for Christ, for it was that the day I was born I was to write about all of Christ glorious wonders. that to this very day man still can't quite understand for only Christ whom which is a holy being NO's all. for I this woman no's that as long as I worshop Christ there is nothing that I can't withstand or endure for my God

Christ will pull me through it all, praise be to God every time the storm approaches me my God Christ steps in and shield's me from any untruth justice for when I'am worshoping him my God Christ stands abrawd right by my side, for I'am only one of his many children and my God Christ will protect his own and so with

That I praise his name again, and again, and again, and as I worshop my lord Christ provides my very being of how to prepare for such awsome authensity and devine living that stands awaiting me in the future of heaven, for I no that my lord Christ is soon to be announced to make that grande awsom appearance that we must

All claim to serve and worshop him in order to make it through those pearly gates of heaven, for we must all no by now we must all stand on one acord, for Christ is judgeing all of us, we must when worshoping God Christ, we must all love one another we must all stand by each others side, we must all praise unto the blessing

Upon one another, we must all and most of all, we must all forgive one another for the love of Christ is indeed forgiveing and aborts any sorrows from our past, for Christ his grace is out standing, nothing can compare to the justification of his mercy, for he has been there when we mourned, when we cryed-out, when we

Were scared, when we were alone, when we plead for help, and must of all when we were lost. for I worshop my God Christ for many reasons, most of all that he cares. He cares enoughf for me and all of his children that he gave his own life that day at calvary that today we may stand another day and forth coming of life. And

As I worshop my lord God Christ, just the thought of that old rugged cross brings tears before my eye's because I no that he bared all for our soles that we may be cleansed some day and that the blood he shead solely for our sins. but low and behold when he roosed the three days later the devil was the one defeated and

Christ plainly, surely, succeeded. and to all of you who are reading this story I want you all to no that this is why I worshop Christ for he is my devine true leader of GOD and this woman halayluya, is none other then me, Ms Donna L Howard PRAISE be unto GOD MY LORD CHRIST IN HEAVEN

THE LORD PRESERVETH THE FAITHFUL
PSALMS 31:32

7-2005

A DISTANT FAMILY

And once upon a time the book end's in a dramatic epic true story telling of how a family that once was seem to just come apart in a way sort to speak all because of such holy devineness that come from a knowledge and wisdom sent only from up above this knowledge and wisdom is to spectacular in its holyness

That the family members of unholy righteousness just seem to stay apart but God said that I may have been enduring for a night and that every thing was going to be allright the next morning for I have friends and love one's in higher place's, that the enemy or the false so to speak can't withstand such awesome anniounting

That has been placed upon my sole you see the light of God shine's, upon me and I have been giving favor overall in my path from non other then God. remember it has also been said that no weapon firmed against me shall prosper, and that no matter what their life stylle's are trouble, worrie's, discomfort, sorrows, pain, grief, financial, the enemy's taken them through, they allway's

Seem yet to call on me. but God said to help a man when he's down and to not let your heart be like the unmerciful, for in thee end that my blessing may be greater in the kingdom of heaven. Yet it is so amazing to me that I have never seen his face. but still yet, all that my God doe's for me is maraculous. but I no that in my heart and sole, behold I shall see his face. O my Lord, O glory

My sweat Lord I shall see your face one day and with that I send praises of worshop to thee because I can never forget that even in my time of weakness he was still there, yes I said still there for me. so I must and I shall seek to do the right things in accordance with my God. for there will be a day that the unrighteous shall give honnor to the work that I bring forth to my Lord

My God for he is using me to let go of my old ways, you see this is how my Lord God use's me, he use's my toung to speak the truth, he use's my voice to sing out loud praise's unto him he use's my hands to lay hand on the sick and afflicted, he use's my legs to walk in the mist of the unrighteous yet never being harmed or hurt. he use's my mind to focus on his spiritual realm,

And he use's my body to bow-down on bended knee's, in given thanks and praise's for all he's done for me, you see God has shown me I have favor overall, and to never dwell on the DISTANT PAST.

GOD LOVETH A CHEERFUL GIVER
11 CORINTHIANS 9:7

8-2005

A PROPHECY

And once upon a time it was written and to be foretold in the book of the lamb that I would go through these task, experiences, trials, and that it was to be told that grande awsom day that I came to realize that it indeed were the foot steps that god had choosen for me to tell of all the world the things that I went through

From a child to learn the hard way about life, from a minor child to learn what it once was for a black nation of people back in grandma's time, from the time that I committed a terrible sin and paid dearly for I was not save then and the devil tryed to take my soul, from the time that I live in a house where a spirit

Dwelled in as a very young woman with a very small child this spirit or intidy of some sort had powers but none of the powers of the glory of god's light that protected me and that small child, from the time that I ran into the man carrying the mark of the beast, with 3" sixe's ingraved in his head, from the time

That I was separated from a torn family because of a drug issue the devil's drug causing family breakdowns, teardowns, letdowns, a drug that would cause you to do just about anything to get to not care, to still, to hate, to beg, to sin, to have no mercy on yourself or other's, from the time I was with a man and his child

Was possessed seeing and witnessing these irrey effect's from his child certainly was truma for me, child with eye's of a demom from the time that I was homeless and experienced what it was like to live without money and to learn that it doesn't take money to survive, eating out trash cans, sleeping park, allies,

Church grounds, taking risk by going into abandon buildings waking up the next morning finding a snake had shead his skin right next to me bowel movements in and out of buckets, bathing in park rest rooms at the break of down trying best to keep clean watching people overdose and brought back to life, husbands and wive's

Asking me to perform a sinful act together with them all because the fact I was homeless, for something to eat or for drug's if I preferd, from the time I finally was baptized in the holy blood of Jesus, and I choose one day to come and let my self be baptize I still experienced awsom things such as God speaking to me telling

Me be stroung Donna be stroung for you will make it in the end I shall never forget his stroung yet frighting beautiful voice of the lamb or lord, from the time I was searching for a real man in my life and God showed me through his devine holyness that there's no true man like unless he's a true man of God,

Praise God, from the time that there came a time in my life in which I was ready and prepared to make something of my self and again God leaded me through the path of in which every thing serve's God and I will prosper, from the time when I was doing so remarkably good that this one day the devil sent a friend by my

House to try and break what God had strenghting within me and you see I was leaded by a friend the most sad part about this task is how our enemy not only would lead you to temptation but also turn his back on you, after going through a nother task of semi homelessness but this time with a child I beg God to help me get back

On my feet and to give me the strength to turn away from my deseatful sinful friends, you see I've ask the lord my savior to put forth new heavenly glorious friends before my presence, from the time a prophet of God wrote me a letter telling me that the Holy spirit was going to come to me, and so it happen and I have

Learned that when living for God the devil tremble's in anger trying to figour ways to break the yoke of God's bond between you and god like he tryed to do to me, from the time that I found Jesus I learned that I really had no true friends and that Jesus indeed is your one and only true friend, and that no matter what

Steps that I was taking he was so there for me and he was my strength, my guide, my comfort, my consolidator, the one that I put my hole strust in him, cause you see by now he never ever left my side, O how I just love him lord GOD I think of his unconditional loving every day that he puts breath into my body,

From the time that my eye's were open wide and God let me see a different kind of life style and let me no that greater is he that believeth in God. And so that when I came to live a life for

Our God,

The most awesom God of all the most awesom king of king's for he is the most high, praise God. O lord I just praise your name, Lord I love you, and most of all from the time that I am now today

Liveing a life purely and simply for Christ, and I totally worshop Christ, for he is my true devine leader of God. For he has shown me so many journey's and now it's time for me to share

My journey's to all, and to let all no that with out him I could have been a lost soul. But low and behold it was prophesied that I would seek these things, and my foot's would walk the step's that Christ laid out before the time I was born.

PRAISE BE TO GOD... you all no that this woman is none other than me. MS. DONNA L, HOWARD

All of These Revelations were Indeed To Take Place Before One Existed In Jesus Holy Name So it was Written So it Shall be Done Amen

WE WILL WALK IN HIS PATH
ISAIAH 2:3

INDEX

To all of you who have read this Book these events are Truth and actual fact Testimonies that took place in my Life for I experience these strange yet unexplainable things Phenomenal things through out my life yet God Leaded me safely through it all and to this Day I give him the Praise the Glory the Thanks for I Magnify him for holding me safely in his Loving Merciful ARMS

AMEN TO GOD /JESUS IN CHRIST

This Book WAS WRITTEN BY MS DONNA LEE HOWARD OF LAS ANGELES CALIFORNIA

THANK YOU JESUS AMEN

REVELATIONS FROM JESUS FROM A YOUNG WOMAN WHO FOUND JESUS

BEHIND EACH STORY THERE IS A SCRIPTURE AND ITS VERSES FROM THE HOLY BIBLE TO GIVE THE READER A VISION OF WHY THAT STORY WAS WRITTEN

THE KINGS JAMES HOLY BIBLE

PRAISE BE TO GOD AMEN

REVELATIONS FROM JESUS TO A YOUNG WOMAN
WHO FOUND JESUS

DECEMBER TWENTY TWENTY TOO
THIS BOOK WAS WRITTEN THE YEAR OF TOO
THOUSAND FIVE IT HAS TAKEN ME THESE MANY
YEARS TO ACHIEVE THE MONEY TO FINALLY
PUBLISH IT YOU SEE FOR I AM TO ONE WHO
LIVES A POOR POVERTY LIFE STYLE GOD BLESS
EVERY ONE AND MAY HE CONTINUE TO SHINE
HIS GLORIOUS LIGHT ON ALL AMEN I LOVE YOU

WE WILL WALK IN HIS PATH
ISAIAH 2:3

Printed in the United States
by Baker & Taylor Publisher Services